WATER POLLUTION

A TRUE BOOK
by
Rhonda Lucas Donald

Children's Press®
A Division of Scholastic Inc.

New York Toronto London Auckland Sydney
Mexico City New Delhi Hong Kong
Danbury, Connecticut

Water is a precious resource that we need to protect and conserve.

Reading Consultant
Linda Cornwell
Coordinator of School Quality
and Professional Improvement
Indiana State Teachers
Association

Content Consultant
Jan Jenner
Rendalia Biologist
Talladega, AL

Author's Dedication:
For Hailey

Library of Congress Cataloging-in-Publication Data

Donald, Rhonda Lucas, 1962–
    Water pollution / by Rhonda Lucas Donald.
        p. cm. — (A true book)
    Includes bibliographical references and index.
    Summary: Explains what water pollution is, how it harms plants and
animals, and how to conserve and protect water.
    ISBN 0-516-22194-9 (lib. bdg.)   0-516-27357-4 (pbk.)
    1. Water—Pollution—Juvenile literature. [1. Water—Pollution.
2. Pollution.] I. Title. II. Series.

TD422 .D657   2001
363.739'4—dc21   00-030839
                                                      CIP
                                                      AC

OCT - - 2002

Contents

The water you use today has been around since the time of the dinosaurs.

Precious Water

Did you know that a dinosaur might have waded in the water you drink today? How? Because our water has been around for millions of years. It is still fresh because it is constantly being recycled. It works like this: Sunlight causes water to evaporate, or dry up, into a gas called

water vapor. The vapor rises into the atmosphere and collects in clouds. When too much water vapor fills the clouds, the vapor condenses back into water and rains down to Earth to begin the cycle again.

Of all the water on the planet, less than 1 percent of it is usable by people. The rest is mostly salt water or is frozen. You can find fresh water in lakes, streams, rivers, and underground in pockets of soil and rock. About half the people in the United States get their water from underground sources. The trouble is, people

Fresh water can be found in lakes, streams, and rivers.

are wasting and polluting our fresh water. Since there is only so much fresh water, it makes sense to protect what we have.

Water Worries

When you think of water pollution, do you think of dirty water coming out of a factory pipe into a stream? Industries do add to water pollution, but they are not the biggest polluters. Most water pollution—as much as 80 percent—comes from things people do every day in their

Factories pollute water (left), but they are not the biggest source of water pollution. Farmers use chemicals that get into the soil and pollute ground water (below).

homes and on farms. Farmers and homeowners put pesticides, weed killers, and fertilizers on their crops and lawns every year to kill unwanted pests and enrich the soil. These chemicals get into the ground and pollute groundwater. When it rains, the chemicals can wash into streams creating polluted runoff. Anything you pour down the drain or dump in the water pollutes it.

What goes up must come down, right? This is true of air-borne pollutants, many of which end up in water. Pollutants from cars and factories rise into the air and mix with water vapor.

These trees have been damaged by acid rain.

When the rain falls, it is acid rain and is harmful to plants, animals, and even buildings. Some pesticides also end up in the air and may travel thousands of miles before settling in streams, lakes, rivers, or the ocean.

Sometimes, a disaster—such as an oil or chemical spill— spoils huge amounts of water and kills plants and wildlife in large numbers. The spill from

Oil spills pollute water and kill plants and wildlife.

the oil tanker *Exxon Valdez* destroyed more than 250,000 animals, billions of fish eggs, and 1,300 miles (2,092 kilometers) of beach. That is as far as from Boston, Massachusetts, to Tampa, Florida. Floods may cause sewers to overflow, forcing out dirty water that ends up in streams or groundwater. Finally, a lot of water is just plain wasted by doing things like letting faucets run when you do not need to or

Dripping faucets waste more water than you think— as much as 20 gallons a day!

taking extra long showers. Everyone needs to respect how precious our water is and learn to conserve it.

What If Water Is Polluted?

Water makes up most of the Earth's surface. Did you know that your body is nearly two-thirds water? The same is true of animals and plants. So if that water is not clean, all living things are at risk.

For example, chemicals such as pesticides that run off

Your body is made mostly of water.

Polluted water is a problem in many countries.

or travel by air collect in water and poison fish and other animals. Even if the animals do not die, the poisons stay in their bodies. When predators eat polluted prey animals, the predators get an even higher dose of the pollutants. Years ago, this happened to birds of prey such as pelicans. DDT, a pesticide, built up in the bodies of the fish and other

Pesticides in the water can poison fish and other animals.

Pelicans were once victims of pollution, but have bounced back.

prey the birds ate. The DDT caused the birds' eggshells to become thin and break, so that they were unable to reproduce. As a result, some became endangered. Since the ban of DDT in 1972, pelicans and other birds of prey have bounced back. As with DDT, pollutants that contaminate groundwater, including pesticides and fertilizers, can build up in peoples' bodies, causing serious diseases such as cancer.

When human and animal wastes get into water, they produce bacteria and viruses that can make anything that drinks or lives in the water sick.

Polluted ground-water can lead to serious diseases.

These wastes can harm water by robbing it of oxygen. If there are too many wastes, water becomes so oxygen poor that fish and other living things cannot survive.

The Wetland Way

The good news is that Earth has its own way of cleaning up dirty water. It is the wetland way.

Wetlands are places that have shallow water or are soggy at least some of the time. Marshes, swamps, tidal flats, prairie potholes, and

Marshes (top), swamps (middle), and tidal flats (bottom) are three ways the Earth cleans up dirty water.

Some wetlands are created by beavers.

bogs are types of wetlands. Some wetlands are even created by beavers when they build their dams. People tend to think of swamps and bogs as dark, damp, scary places.

Herons (top), egrets (bottom left), and crabs (bottom right) are just three of the many species that make their homes in wetlands.

The truth is, wetlands are habitats with a lot of life in them that do a great job of cleaning our water and preventing flooding.

Wetlands act like giant sponges, soaking up and holding lots of water that might otherwise flood surrounding areas. In the process of holding the water, wetlands also help clean it up. Plant roots trap mud and soak up pollutants in the water, leaving it cleaner

This beach has been eroded by waves.

when it finally seeps into groundwater. If there were no wetlands, all that mud would end up in streams, rivers, lakes, or the ocean and could kill fish and other animals. Have you ever been to a beach that has been eroded by the waves? Wetlands are natural barriers to erosion, holding on to the soil or sand so that it does not wash away.

The bad news is that people have destroyed many of Earth's wetlands by filling them in to build homes, businesses, and recreational areas. More than half of the United States' wetlands are already gone, and more are lost every year. Slowly, people are

Parts of Washington, D.C., are built on a former wetland.

realizing how important these soggy places are, and the government has passed laws to protect more wetlands.

How a Wetland Works

Here is a demonstration of how a wetland traps pollution. Put a sponge into one end of a shallow pan. Make sure it reaches all the way from one side of the pan to the other. Add a spoon of dirt to a cup of water and stir. Slowly pour a small amount of the dirty water onto the sponge, and tip the pan so that the water runs through the sponge into the other end of the pan. Pour the "runoff" into another cup and compare it with the dirty water. It is cleaner because the sponge, like a wetland, traps and holds some of the dirt. But real wetlands do a much better job than a sponge!

Help Clean Up Our Water

In the early 1970s, people got a wake-up call about water pollution: Lake Erie had become so polluted that it actually caught on fire! Other lakes, rivers, and streams were almost as bad. In response, Congress passed the Clean Water Act in

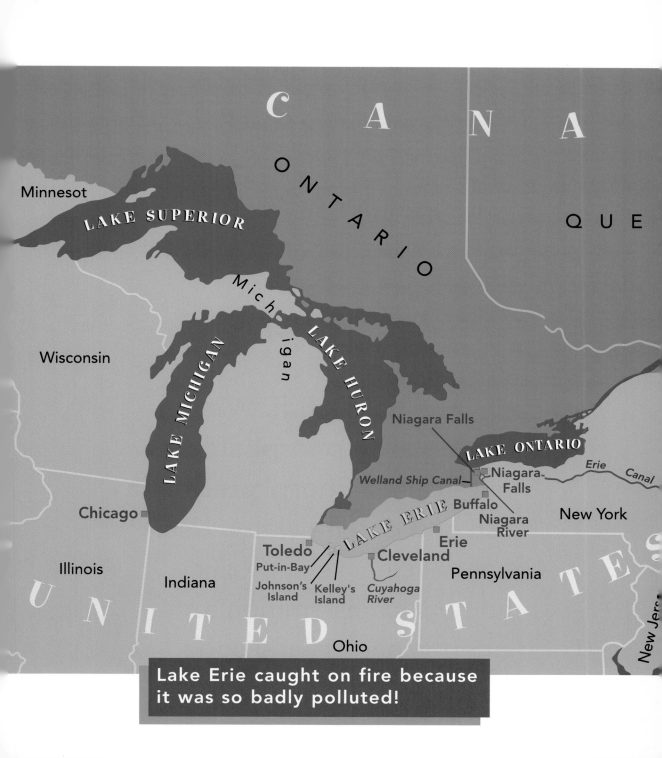

Lake Erie caught on fire because it was so badly polluted!

1972, which has helped clean up dirty waters and prevent water pollution. While things have improved a lot, we still have a way to go.

There are lots of things you can do to help.

• Use safer stuff. Wash laundry with phosphate-free detergents. Phosphates harm fish and pollute water. Use natural cleansers in your home such as ammonia, vinegar, and baking soda.

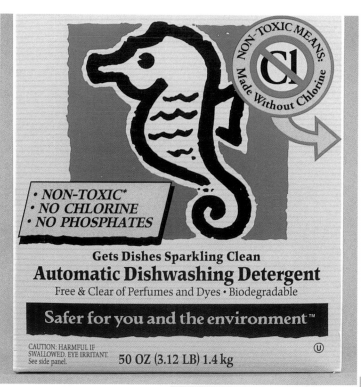

- *NON-TOXIC*
- *NO CHLORINE*
- *NO PHOSPHATES*

NON-TOXIC MEANS: Made Without Chlorine

Gets Dishes Sparkling Clean
Automatic Dishwashing Detergent
Free & Clear of Perfumes and Dyes • Biodegradable

Safer for you and the environment™

CAUTION: HARMFUL IF
SWALLOWED. EYE IRRITANT.
See side panel.   50 OZ (3.12 LB) 1.4 kg

Phosphate-free
detergent (above)
and natural
cleansers (right).

Insect and weed killers.

Avoid using pesticides,
weed killers, and chemical
fertilizers.

• Do not dump it. Never dump paints, oil, or chemicals down the drain. Call your trash collector and ask how to recycle or dispose of these poisons safely.

Dispose of toxic trash safely so poisons do not end up in our water.

Put water in the refrigerator to get it cold instead of running the faucet.

• Waste not. Do not run the water to get it hot or cold. Fill a pitcher and put it in the refrigerator to keep it cold, and let the stove do the heating.

Repair leaky faucets or toilets right away. Only water the yard when it really needs it, and then do it in the early morning. Sweep off walks and outdoor steps instead of hosing them down.

Use brooms to sweep walkways instead of hosing them down.

Start a compost pile to use up kitchen wastes instead of running the disposal—and the water—to get rid of them. A compost pile is a place to put kitchen scraps, leaves, grass, and yard trimmings to rot. Use a shovel to mix up the stuff every week, and in several weeks these wastes will turn into rich compost to add to your soil. The compost-improved soil also holds water better so you won't have to water as much.

If we all pitch in and do our part, we can keep our water clean.

Kids Watch the Water

The Elkhart River Scientists are a small group of third through fifth graders in Goshen, Indiana, who do a big job to protect the Elkhart River habitat. The kids test the water for pollution and report results to the Department of Natural Resources.

The Elkhart River Scientists in Goshen, Indiana.

They also work with scientists at the University of Notre Dame to monitor the ruffe, a species of fish that got in the river accidentally and caused trouble for native fish. The Scientists helped raise money to bring otters back to the river. Now these animals once again frolic in a great otter habitat.

To Find Out More

To learn more about water pollution, check out these resources.

 **Books**

Costa-Pau, Rosa; Elvira Soriano; and Jordi Segu. **Protecting Our Rivers and Lakes.** Chelsea House Publishers, 1994.

Hoff, Mary King. **Our Endangered Planet: Groundwater** and **Our Endangered Planet: Rivers and Lakes.** Lerner Publications, 1991.

Lampton, Christopher. **Oil Spill.** Millbrook Press, 1994.

Santore, Charles. **William the Curious: Knight of the Water Lilies.** Random House, 1997.

Snodgrass, Mary Ellen. **Environmental Awareness: Water Pollution.** Bancroft-Sage Publishing, 1991.

Stille, Darlene R. **Wetlands.** Children's Press, 1999.

Organizations and Online Sites

The Groundwater Foundation
5561 S. 48th, Ste. 215
Lincoln, NE 68516
*www.groundwater.org/
KidsCorner/kidscorner.htm*

This Web site contains games and puzzles, and ideas on how to protect and conserve groundwater.

Environmental Protection Agency (EPA)
Public Information Center
401 M St., SW (TM-211B)
Washington, DC 20460
*www.epa.gov/OGWDW/
kids*

The Kid's Page of the EPA Web site has information and activities about groundwater and drinking water.

The Natural Resources Defense Council
40 West 20th St.
New York, NY 10011
www.nrdc.org

You can request a free copy of the Earth Action Guide "What You Can Do to Keep Our Water Safe and Clean" on the Web site.

University of Wisconsin Cooperative Extension
www.uwex.edu/erc/gwah

At this Web site, you can download the "Give Water a Hand Action Guide," which contains lots of ideas for protecting our water.

Important Words

atmosphere the layer of air that surrounds Earth

cancer a disease in which harmful growths spread in the body

condensation formation of water droplets from water vapor

erosion wearing away of something, such as a beach from the action of waves or storms

evaporate to change into a gas or vapor

prairie potholes marshes and wet meadows dotted throughout the Midwest and into Canada

runoff rain, snow, or other water that runs off land and into streams, rivers, and other water sources. Runoff can pick up and carry pollutants with it.

Index

Meet the Author

Rhonda Lucas Donald has written for children and teachers for fifteen years. Her work has appeared in magazines such as *Ranger Rick* and *Your Big Backyard*. She specializes in writing about science and natural history and creating projects that make these subjects fun. Rhonda received the EdPress award for best newsletter of 1997 for *EarthSavers*, an environmental newspaper and activity guide. She has also written several other environmental True Books for Children's Press. She

lives in North Carolina with her husband Bruce, cats Sophie and Tory, and Maggie the dog.